Shrinking Powder

Roderick Hunt • Alex Brychta

OXFORD
UNIVERSITY PRESS

Dad did the washing, but he put
the clothes in a hot wash.

"Oh no!" said Dad. "The clothes
have shrunk."

"Look at my top," said Kipper.

"Look at my jeans," said Biff.

"Sorry," said Dad. "I forgot to set
the washing machine. It was too hot."

Chip made a little boy with the
clothes that had shrunk.

"That's a good joke," laughed Biff.

Suddenly, the magic key began to glow. It took the children into an adventure.

The key took them to a shop.
It sold magic tricks and strange
things.

"Wow!" said Chip. "It's a joke
shop. But there's nobody here.
I think the shop is shut."

Suddenly, there was a loud POP
and a puff of purple smoke.
"What's that?" asked Chip.

A boy was standing in the shop.
"I'm sorry about all the smoke,"
he said.

"I'm Jake," said the boy. "I'm
learning to be a wizard. Watch
this."

"Hooray! It works," said Jake,
"but learning to be a wizard is not
easy."

Jake took a tin out of his pocket.
"I want to try this," he said.

"It's shrinking powder," said Jake.
"I want to see if it works."

He shook some over Kipper.

Kipper began to shrink. "Help!"
he said. "Everything looks big."

"Hooray!" said Jake. "It works!"

"Oh no!" said Biff and Chip.

"Kipper has shrunk."

"It's not funny," said Kipper.

Jake tapped Kipper with a wand.

"Now I'll make him big," he said.

Suddenly, Kipper had huge ears.
"Whoops!" said Jake. "That's not
quite right ... let me try again."

Jake waved the wand. Suddenly,
Kipper had long, green hair.

"This is *not* funny," said Kipper.

Jake waved the wand again.

"I *am* sorry," said Jake. "I can't make him big."

Chip was cross. He took Jake's
wand. "Let *me* try," he said.
Just then, the key glowed.

The key took them back. Kipper's big ears and green hair had gone, but he was still small.

"Dad is coming," said Chip. "We can't let him see Kipper."

"Let's put a box on him," said Biff.

Suddenly, Kipper was big again.
"What are you up to?" asked Dad.

"Shrinking Kipper," said Biff.

"That's a good joke!" laughed
Dad.

Think about the story

Jake's mistakes – rhyming pairs

Jake has put the wrong labels on the pictures.
Can you find the right ones?

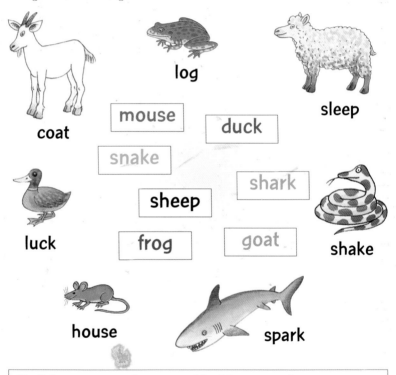

coat

log

sleep

mouse

duck

snake

shark

sheep

luck

frog

goat

shake

house

spark